Why the USS THRESHER (SSN 593) Was Lost

A Technical Assessment Based on Analyses of Acoustic Detections of the Event

An Introductory Note

The purpose of this technical assessment is to inform Naval historians and acoustic analysts at the Office of Naval Intelligence and elsewhere of the results of analyses of acoustic detections of the loss of the USS THRESHER. That analysis has identified conditions responsible for the disaster which occurred more than half a century ago. Loss of the USS SCORPION is discussed as that event relates to the loss of THRESHER and -generically - to analyses of acoustic detections of submarine pressure-hull collapse events.

This technical assessment has not been written in the format commonly used for discussions of such events, i.e., there is no narrative continuity, only discussions of the analysis techniques used and the information derived. The persevering general reader should also find this information of value.

Summary

Refined analysis in 2009 of the original acoustic detections of the loss of the USS THRESHER (SSN 593) on 10 April 1963 confirmed the pressure-hull and all sea connected systems survived intact - without flooding - until collapse at a depth of 2400-feet, almost twice test-depth (1300-feet). Based on multiple lines of evidence discussed in detail by this assessment, the 1963 conclusion by the Navy Court of Inquiry that flooding at test-depth occurred because of faulty silver brazing of a joint in a sea-connected pipe between two- and five-inches in diameter is disproven. Portsmouth Naval Shipyard personnel are thus exculpated of any complicity in the tragedy. Indeed, they "built better than they knew."

Loss of propulsion (reactor scram) for a still unknown cause (NOT flooding), failure to compensate for hull-compression from increasing pressure during the dive to test-depth (1300-feet), and failure of the deballasting system because of the formation of ice in the air-lines were the primary factors responsible for the loss of THRESHER.

Bruce Rule

Nimble Books LLC

Table of Contents

Nimble Books LLC

Author's Bona Fides

As the Analysis Officer at the Sound Surveillance System (SOSUS) Evaluation Center in 1962-63, the author analyzed SOSUS detections of the loss of THRESHER, testified before the Navy Court of Inquiry in closed session on 18 April 1963, and subsequently was the lead acoustic analyst at the Office of Naval Intelligence - the national laboratory for the exploitation of passively-collected acoustic data - for 42 years.

Two weeks prior to the loss of THRESHER, the author finished writing and the Navy published "THE US NUCLEAR SUBMARINE ACOUSTIC DATA HANDBOOK," a classified summary of information derived from the author's analytical review of all SOSUS detections of US nuclear submarines from 1958 to March 1963 including detections of THRESHER prior to overhaul. Those data included several hundred hours of acoustic detections of Main Coolant Pump sources from submarines with SSW reactor systems -installed in THRESHER - in both FAST- and SLOW-speed operating modes.

In 2003, the author provided technical (analytical) support to the David Taylor Naval Ship Research and Development Center (DTNSRDC), the activity responsible for US Nuclear Submarine Noise Trials. That support involved documentation of the passive acoustic target classification potential of a US nuclear submarine acoustic characteristic of which DTNSRDC was not aware.

In 2008, the author analyzed acoustic data from the public domain to confirm the USS SCORPION (SSN 589) was lost at 18:42:34Z on 22 May 1968 because hydrogen out-gassed by the main battery exploded. In 2011, the results of this analysis -the first review of SCORPION acoustic data in 40 years - were published as WHY THE USS SCORPION (SSN 589) WAS LOST, ISBN 978-1-60888-120-8. Royalties from the SCORPION book were declined as will royalties from this book.

In 2009, the author analyzed acoustic data to determine- for the first time at any security level - that the GOLF-II Class Soviet ballistic missile submarine (SSB) K-129 was lost on 11 March 1968 because two R-21/D4 ballistic missiles fired to fuel exhaustion within the pressure-hull killing the crew and causing enormous structural damage. Acoustic-derived full-thrust missile firing durations of 95.2 and 95.4 seconds and an ignition interval of 361 seconds were subsequently confirmed by a Russian source for the R-21/D4 system as "about 94 seconds" and "six minutes" (360 seconds).

This Technical Assessment Was Written to:

1. Document that the intact THRESHER (SSN 593) pressure-hull was completely destroyed at a depth of 2400-feet by hydrostatic pressure (1070 psi) in 1/20th of a second, too fast to be cognitively recognized by those aboard who- although they knew the event was imminent- never knew it was occurring.

2. Establish that the Portsmouth Naval Shipyard personnel built a pressure hull that survived-without flooding- to nearly twice test-depth. Those personnel were not complicit in any way in the loss of THRESHER. This information for the special attention of the Historian, Portsmouth Naval Shipyard, and for other individuals and activities concerned with the loss of THRESHER specifically or with naval history generally.

3. Provide - in one open source document - what is known about the temporal and dynamic characteristics of submarine pressure-hull collapse events including information identified for the first time during the analysis effort reported by this assessment.

4. Disprove the THRESHER Court of Inquiry conclusion that flooding caused THRESHER to lose propulsion and thus was the proximate cause of the disaster.

5. Establish the probability that actions/inactions by the crew (failure to compensate for hull-compression with depth and operation of the Main Coolant Pumps in FAST), and then-extant operational procedures contributed to the loss of THRESHER, i.e, no authorization to use residual heat to provide limited post-scram propulsion.

6. Identify - and refute - erroneous information in the public domain about the loss of THRESHER. (See Appendix A)

7. Provide acoustic analysts with a method for distinguishing acoustic detections of explosions from implosions.

8. As an ancillary issue, disprove the basic conclusion by the SCORPION Court of Inquiry that SCORPION (SSN 589) was lost because of the "explosion of a large charge weight external to the pressure-hull," and confirm that the cause of that disaster was the explosion - contained within the pressure-hull - of hydrogen out-gassed by the main battery, an assessment provided to the Court of Inquiry in 1969 by their own team of technical experts but which the Court of Inquiry rejected. Additionally, explain why the SCORPION propeller shaft separated from the hull. (See Appendix C)

Additional Notes to the Reader

The unusual organization of this technical assessment - six summary assessments followed by three chapters and four appendices - developed from the need to include previously published "stand-alone" technical monographs written over a four-year period- as components of a single document, and the requirement to increase the "visibility" of critically important information such as the full explanation of THRESHER's last UQC ("underwater telephone") transmission: "900 North," which is arguably- in its full explanation- the most important information provided by this technical assessment. That explanation alone refutes the basic conclusion by the Navy Court of Inquiry that flooding occurred before collapse of the THRESHER pressure-hull and thus was the proximate cause of the tragedy.

Each of these monographs (Chapters 1-3 and Appendices A-D) discuss distinctly separate issues related to the loss of the USS THRESHER (SSN 593) and the loss of the USS SCORPION (SSN 589) as that event relates to the loss of THRESHER. Because their technical content supports conclusions provided by other Chapters and Appendices, selected contents are reprised elsewhere as useful.

Unavoidably, this method of insuring relevant information is provided wherever needed in both the summary assessments and the Chapters/Appendices- and the use of monographs written at different times - results in the repetition of basic conclusions about the cause of the THRESHER tragedy and the analysis methods used to derive those conclusions. Such repetition usefully serves to emphasize the conclusion that the Navy has not, in more than half a century, acknowledged there was no flooding prior to collapse of the THRESHER pressure-hull at great depth. Prime among these oft repeated statements is that THRESHER never reported "flooding" to her escort ship, the USS SKYLARK.

Appendix B, "Why the Legacy of the SCORPION Court of Inquiry is Misinformation," has been included in this THRESHER assessment to provide examples of the basic errors that can be made during analyses of acoustic detections of submarine pressure-hull collapse events and to provide information useful in assessing aspects of collapse-associated events evident in imagery of wreckage for which there may be no coincident acoustic data, e.g., the temporal dynamics of- and the forces involved in - collapse events that occur at great depth.

Appendix C has been included in this assessment to resolve a long-standing issue: why the SCORPION propeller shaft was ejected from the hull (cause or effect of the disaster?) and to quantify the enormous destructive forces associated with the collapse of submarine pressure-hulls at great depth.

Appendix D has been included in this assessment to archive and provide reference to useful information on hydrostatic collapse experiments that otherwise might not be available to support analyses of acoustic detections of any future submarine pressure-hull collapse events.

Special note to the reader: event times in this document are times of occurrence onboard THRESHER, i.e., acoustic detection times have been corrected for sound-travel-time (circa 36 seconds) from the wreck-site to the detecting acoustic sensor.

For those readers more concerned with the basic conclusions provided by this technical assessment about the loss of THRESHER than with the complex analyses from which these conclusions were derived, it is suggested they first read the Epilogue on the last two pages of this assessment.

Background

The USS THRESHER (SSN-593) was the lead hull of a new class of attack nuclear submarine designed to provide great advances in quieting, sonar performance (BQQ-2) and depth capabilities: a maximum of 1300-feet, almost twice the capability of the earlier class of SSN, the USS SKIPJACK (SSN 585).

The keel was laid down on 28 May 1958 at the Portsmouth Naval Shipyard, Portsmouth, NH. She was launched on 9 July 1960, and commissioned on 3 August 1961. Her normal complement was 112: 16 officers and 96 enlisted. When lost, there were 17 additional personnel aboard for a total of 129.

THRESHER returned to Portsmouth Naval Shipyard on 16 July 1962 to begin a scheduled 6-month, post-shakedown availability to examine systems and make repairs and corrections as necessary. After nine months, THRESHER was recertified and left for sea trials on 9 April 1963 which were to include a dive to test-depth (1300-feet) on 10 April.

When THRESHER was lost in the western North Atlantic (near 41-45N, 65-00W) during the scheduled dive to test-depth, the collapse (implosion) of the pressure hull at great depth produced a powerful pulse of acoustic energy detected by every Sound Surveillance System (SOSUS) hydrophone array then operational in the Atlantic. Detection ranges were between 30 and 1300 nautical miles. (Reflections - 'echoes" - of the collapse signal from the mid-Atlantic Ridge were detected by several SOSUS arrays,) The signal-to-noise ratio of the collapse signal assessed at 1300 miles indicated it could have been acoustically detected at ranges equal to the circumference of the earth; however, the greatest range for which an unobstructed deep-water transmission path existed was 10,160 nautical miles where the signal would have "run-out" of continuous deep-water near the southern coast of Australia: 33S, 123E.

Analyses of the SOSUS data - presented to the THRESHER Court of Inquiry (COI) on 18 April 1963 by the author- confirmed a loss of electrical power and the resulting reactor scram (shut-down) at the now established local time of 0909.0R at or near test-depth (1300-feet), about nine minutes before collapse of the pressure-hull. In 2009, refined analysis of the collapse event acoustic signal confirmed it occurred at a depth of 2400-feet with an energy release equal to the explosion of 22,500 lbs of TNT at that depth, the result of the nearly instantaneous conversion of potential energy (sea pressure of 1070 psi) to kinetic energy, the motion of the water-ram into the collapsing pressure-hull at a speed of 2600 mph.

In summary, this technical assessment - in the form of multiple monographs - discusses the results of those analysis efforts and communications between

THRESHER and her escort ship, the USS SKYLARK (ASR 20), that confirm there was no flooding before collapse of the pressure-hull. These determinations provide the basis for rejecting the Court of Inquiry conclusion that flooding was the proximate cause of the disaster.

Dedication

This technical assessment is dedicated to those few Portsmouth Naval Shipyard (PNSY) personnel still living - and those now deceased - who - for more than 50 years- have been implicated by the Navy in the loss of the USS THRESHER, and to whom - including the relatives of those deceased - the Navy owes a public apology for that often repeated erroneous assessment that flooding occurred at test-depth (1300-feet) because of faulty silver-brazing (1) in a sea-connected system.

The evidence is overwhelming that those PNSY personnel "built better than they knew" and should have been commended for having done so. The THRESHER pressure-hull and all sea-connected systems survived without breach to almost twice test-depth: 2400-feet (1070 psi sea pressure). (See Chapter 1)

NlliːEIːE>E THN AAHE>EIAN KAI H AAHE>EIA EAEYE>EPOIːEI YMAI:

("You shall know the truth and the truth shall make you free.")

(1) Silver-brazing is a joining process where a non-ferrous filler metal alloy is heated to melting temperature and distributed between two close-fitting components by capillary attraction.

Perspective

This technical assessment of the loss of the USS THRESHER, and a companion assessment, "Why the USS SCORPION (SSN 589) Was Lost" (Nimble Books LLC, ISBN 978-1-60888-120-8, 31 Oct 2011), have been written to inform Naval historians, intelligence analysts and - especially - acoustic analysts that the THRESHER and SCORPION Navy Courts of Inquiry did not correctly evaluate the acoustic data that has proven crucial to understanding why these disasters occurred. Those erroneous Court of Inquiry assessments are still- after half a century - the official Navy explanations for these disasters.

The first erroneous assessment was that Portsmouth Naval Shipyard personnel were complicit in the loss of THRESHER because of faulty silver-brazing of a joint in a sea-connected pipe, the failure of which caused flooding and a loss of propulsion at a depth of 1300-feet. That assessment was officially made in 1963 - and was still maintained in 2016 - even though the Court of Inquiry's own test in 1963 - and analysis in 2009 of acoustic detections of the THRESHER collapse-event signal confirmed there was no flooding before collapse of the pressure-hull at a depth of
2400-feet. (See Chapter 1).

Another erroneous assessment was the SCORPION COI's dismissal of the conclusion by their own team of technical experts - the Structural Analysis Group (SAG) - that the major acoustic event (signal) that occurred at 18:42:34Z (GMT) on 22 May 1968 in the east central Atlantic (32-55N,33-09W) was collapse of the SCORPION pressure-hull. The COI concluded that event was produced by the "explosion of a large charge weight external to the pressure-hull," an error that was generatively responsible for conspiracy theories that SCORPION was sunk by a Soviet torpedo. The SAG assessment was validated in 2009 by confirmation that the energy-level of that signal - equal to the explosion of 13,200 lbs of TNT - could only have been produced by hull-collapse.

The SCORPION Court of Inquiry also rejected the SAG's correct conclusion that a "precursor" acoustic signal detected 21 minutes and 50 seconds minutes before collapse was the explosion of hydrogen out-gassed by the main battery, the proximate cause of the disaster as confirmed by metalurgical analysis of battery components recovered from the wreck site by the US Submersible TRIESTE..

Chapter 3 of this technical assessment discusses an analysis technique that has the potential to acoustically distinguish underwater explosions from implosions (collapse events). That criteria is based on analysis of a recording of acoustic detection of the SCORPION collapse-event which occurred in 0.037 seconds at a depth of 1530-feet. Information provided by Appendix D supports this technical assessment.

Nimble Books LLC

Timeline of THRESHER-Associated Events and Derived Conclusions

Analysis of Sound Surveillance System (SOSUS) acoustic detections of the loss of the USS THRESHER (SSN-593) on 10 April 1963 confirms the following timeline of events, all times local (ROMEO).

0909.0: Loss of propulsion power (reactor scram) coincident with a loss of non vital bus electrical system line-frequency stability while THRESHER was at or near test-depth: 1300-feet. Verified operation of the Main Coolant Pumps (MCPs) in high-speed (FAST) mode meant the battery-powered back-up electrical system (the vital bus) could not accept the electrical load pf MCPs in FAST; the MCPs failed, and the nuclear reactor scrammed with the resulting loss of propulsion.

0909.8: THRESHER initiated an attempt to deballast which failed due to the formation of ice in the air lines: adiabatic cooling effect. Had THRESHER retained propulsion, that attempt to deballast would not have been necessary. THRESHER could have used propulsion to drive to the surface. The attempt to deballast only 48 seconds after loss of propulsion suggests increasing depth had become evident in that short period which further suggests THRESHER had been operating at a speed low enough to lose depth-maintaining momentum in that period, i.e., probably less than five knots.

0913: Using UQC ("underwater telephone"), THRESHER informed her escort ship, the USS SKYLARK (ASR-20) that she was "experiencing minor difficulties." Court of Inquiry (COI) tests confirmed the effects of flooding at test-depth -the COI's assessed cause of the disaster - would have been catastrophic, preventing communications which continued intermittently until 0917. THRESHER never mentioned "flooding" in any communications with SKYLARK. (See Appendix A.)

0917: THRESHER transmitted "900 North," an indirect reference -as required for security- to depth: 900 feet below test-depth or 2200-feet.

09:18:24: THRESHER's pressure-hull collapsed at a depth of 2400-feet (1070 psi) with an energy release equal to the explosion of 22,500 lbs of TNT at that depth. Complete destruction occurred in 1/20th of a second, too fast to be cognitively recognized by those aboard.

The sink-rate, an average of 120-feet a minute- from 1300-feet at 0909.0R to collapse 9.5 minutes later at 2400-feet without flooding- is attributed to failure to compensate for hull compression with increasing depth which allowed THRESHER to reach test-depth at least 12,000 pounds heavy overall.

As previously noted, in 1963, the THRESHER Court of Inquiry erroneously concluded the rupture of a sea-connected pipe between two and five inches in diameter at test depth was the proximate cause for the loss of THRESHER. The THRESHER pressure-hull actually survived without flooding (any breach) to almost twice test depth: 2400-feet.

Nimble Books LLC

Acknowledgements

The author is indebted to the following individuals for information and support that provided the basis for several of the technical assessments included in this book.

Stephen Johnson whose research for "SILENT STEEL: THE MYSTERIOUS DEATH OF THE NUCLEAR ATIACK SUB SCORPION" set the standard for accuracy and detail, and which allowed this author to not only refute conspiracy theories about and official misinformation on that tragedy but which also provided the basis for determining the temporal and dynamic characteristics of the collapse of the THRESHER pressure-hull.

George Miller who reviewed several drafts of this assessment and provided many useful technical and organization suggestions, all of which were implemented.

Chuck Baker who calculated the collapse depth and energy release values for THRESHER and SCORPION based on analyses of acoustic data.

Harold Evans, a consulting engineer, who calculated intruding water-ram velocities for THRESHER at various depths and provided many useful comments/observations.

Dennis Mosebey for supportive comments, suggestions and editing.

Stephen Walsh, who provided valuable technical information on submarine design characteristics and operating procedures. Mr. Walsh, a retired civilian engineer working for the U.S. Navy for nearly 39 years, started that career by working as a Naval Architect at Portsmouth Naval Shipyard (submarine hydrostatics). He later worked at the Naval Sea Systems Command as a Naval Architect on submarine hydrostatics; as a Project Engineer (Deep Submergence Vehicles (DSVs)); as a Assistant Program Manager (APM) managing a number of Deep Submergence assets (e.g. the DSVs, Submarine NR-1, USS DOLPHIN (AGSS 555), a number of unmanned vehicles (UMV's), and the U.S. Navy's Submarine Escape, Survivability and Rescue- including the Deep Submergence Rescue Vehicles (DSRVs) and Submarine Rescue Chambers (SRCs). As an APM, he later delivered the U.S. Navy SEAL Advanced SEAL Delivery System (ASDS) to the SEALs and managed the in-service SEALs Dry Deck Shelter (DDS) Program and the integration of these assets, and other SEAL capabilities onto the USN SSN and SSGN Submarines.

An engineer who cannot be identified at this time, who calculated flooding rates for THRESHER through two-inch and five-inch diameter pipes at test-depth.

Norman Polmar, an accomplished naval analyst, historian and author, who first published the THRESHER collapse depth assessment of 2400-feet in his NAVY

TIMES article of 4 April 2013, That value was also discussed in the April 2013 issue of The PING, The Submarine Force Library and Museum Newsletter. The NAVY TIMES article is available at http://www.iusscaa.org/articles/brucerule/uss thresher (ssn-593) article in the 4 apr 2013 issus of navy times.htm

Others who cannot be identified at this time, who provided critically important technical information on nuclear submarine design and operations at test depth.

Daniel McMillin (1929-2015), an electrical and mechanical engineer who was part of the AT&T Bell Labs "brain trust" involved in the development and evolution of the Navy's Sound Surveillance System, and who provided the author with the USS SCORPION acoustic data. Those data established the relative durations of the compression and expansion phases of the collapse of a submarine pressure hull. That information was used to determine the THRESHER pressure-hull was destroyed in 1120th of a second.

Frank Gambino (1931-2015), a former analyst at the SOSUS Data Processing Unit, New York Naval Shipyard who, in 2011, advise the author that reflections (echoes) of the THRESHER collapse event signal from the Mid-Atlantic Ridge had been detected by SOSUS arrays in the Western Atlantic Basin.

And finally, thanks unlimited to my wife, Mary Cameron Goodwyn, for enduring what must have often appeared to be my unending preoccupation with SCORPION, THRESHER and the GOLF II Class Soviet SSB K-129 which - with the publication of this book- has now ended.

Nimble Books LLC

"900 North"

That phrase was THRESHER's last UQC ("underwater telephone") transmission - at 0917R on 10 April 1963 - to her escort ship, the USS SKYLARK (ASR 20). The meaning of that transmission was confirmed in 2009 when refined analysis of THRESHER's collapse-event acoustic signal established the event occurred at a depth of 2400-feet (1070 psi) at 09:18:24R.

At 0752R, THRESHER advised SKYLARK, via UQC, that her depth was 400- feet. At 0754R, THRESHER further advised SKYLARK that (for security reasons) all future references to depth would be given relative to test depth. (1) The number "900" was thus an indirect reference by THRESHER to her depth at 0917R: 900 feet below her test-depth of 1300-feet or 2200-feet. The word "North" is assessed to have been a direction. In this case "up" as north is on all maps, i.e., test-depth was above THRESHER by 900-feet at 0917R

It is concluded this obvious explanation for the phrase "900 North" was dismissed in 1963 by the THRESHER Court of Inquiry because it required the THRESHER pressure-hull to already have survived to a depth 250-feet greater than the estimated collapse depth of 1950-feet.

Additionally, this explanation for "900 North" would have invalidated the conclusion that flooding had occurred at test-depth (1300-feet) because - if the Court of Inquiry had calculated flooding rates through a breached, sea connected pipe between two and five inches in diameter - which they assessed to have been the case - the Court of Inquiry would have realized that during the 0911-0917 period (Court of Inquiry conjectured time of the reactor scram due to flooding to the time of the "900 North" UQC transmission), flooding would have added more than 100,000 pounds in water-weight (two-inch pipe) or more than 600,000 pounds (five-inch pipe). (See Issue A in Chapter 1)

And finally, it was not credible in 1963 - nor is it credible in 2017 - that THRESHER - had she already experienced catastrophic flooding for six minutes
- would have transmitted a depth value at 0917R- about 90-seconds before collapse of the pressure-hull - without previously having made any mention of flooding to SKYLARK. (See Chapter 1, Issue A)

The last word on this issue should belong to THRESHER, and that last word - at 0917R - was NOT "flooding," it was "900 North" (my depth is 2200-feet). (See Appendix A)

(1) https://books.google.com/books"?
id=d9CkAwAAQBAJ&pg=PA21O&lpg=PA21O&dg=thresher+skylark+ugc+e
xchanges&source=bl&ots=VTRL4a6Q2R&sig=t7NBoSl
OQgH9Lplw7aYKjMQbtM&hl=en&sa=X&ved=OahUKEwiup52L5tXPAhWF
WT4KHesQAJ4Q6AEIJzAC#v=onepage&g=thresher%20skylark%20ugc
%20exchanges&f=false (page 210)

What the THRESHER Court of Inquiry
Should Have Known But Apparently Dismissed

The THRESHER Court of Inquiry Finding of Fact (FoF) 153 provides compelling support for the conclusion there was no flooding before collapse of the pressure-hull at 09:18:24R on 10 April 1963. FoF 153 states: (quote) That during the course of proceedings, a test demonstration for the Court of Inquiry was held in Drydock No. 2 at the Portsmouth Naval Shipyard. A stream of water was released to atmosphere at Thresher's test-depth pressure (580 psi) against a piece of electronic equipment. The stream produced tremendous force, spray, fog and noise. (end quote) Those conditions would not have been reported by THRESHER to her escort ship, the USS SKYLARK (ASR-20) as (quote) experiencing minor difficulties (end quote).

Russell Preble, CDR USN (ret), who was at the Portsmouth Naval Shipyard in April 1963, and who actually observed that test, made the following statement: (quote) A memory that stands out in my mind was watching one of the Board of Inquiry's tests. An old SS radar console was placed on the floor of one of the empty dry docks and a high pressure stream of water was directed against the console. The noise was overwhelming. I remember thinking that nothing could be heard over the noise of the water smashing up against the radar casing and how at deep submergence no orders could be heard over the roar of water striking anything in its way. (end quote) (Reference: "USS Thresher, Lest We Forget", Burke Consortium, Inc, 2013, p. 5; file name: ThresherBooklet_printv2.pdf)

Thus the Court of Inquiry should have known that the flooding they postulated to have been the cause of the loss of THRESHER would have made underwater (UQC) communications with her escort ship, the USS SKYLARK, essentially impossible; however, those communications continued intermittently until 0917R, four minutes after THRESHER reported "experiencing minor difficulty." As previously stated, THRESHER never mentioned "flooding" in any communications with SKYLARK, even that apparently complete transmission at 0913R, four minutes after the acoustic-based assessment of loss of propulsion at 0909.0Z: the reactor scram.

Note: In 1963, the THRESHER Court of Inquiry concluded propulsion was lost two minutes later: at 0911.0R. (See Appendix A)

CHAPTER 1

Why the USS THRESHER (SSN 593) Was Lost

Nimble Books LLC

Monograph of 10 April 2016

Subj: Why the USS THRESHER {SSN-593) Was Lost

PREFACE

In 1974, 76 years after the US Battleship MAINE sank in Havana harbor, an event then attributed to a Cuban or Spanish mine, ADM H. G. Rickover directed a re-examination of photographs taken of the wreckage when it became available for inspection in 1911. That review determined that "an internally initiated explosion had destroyed the MAINE." (Reference: 'How The Battleship MAINE Was Destroyed," by H. G. Rickover, 1995 Edition, Naval Institute Press)

In anticipation of at least a similar hiatus before the Navy may formally review the 1963 Findings of the THRESHER Court of Inquiry, this document provides acoustic-based information related to the event that could otherwise become "perishable" (lost) and unavailable to support future assessments.

In 1963, Vice Adm. H.G. Rickover, at the time head of the Navy's nuclear propulsion program, told Congress:

"When fact, supposition and speculation, which have been used interchangeably, are properly separated, you will find that the known facts are so meager it is almost impossible to tell what was happening aboard Thresher."

When the temporal facts surrounding the loss of THRESHER are examined, the single fact that supports sea water system flooding as the cause is the fact that the ship sank. All other observable facts are derived from acoustic information and **NONE** support sea water system failure as the primary cause of the disaster. (See issue A below)

WHY THRESHER WAS LOST

The following is a summary of THRESHER's UQC transmissions to the USS SKYLARK and events with associated times derived from analyses of acoustic data: Sound Surveillance System {SOSUS) detections made at a range of 30 nautical miles.

0752R: THRESHER reported to her escort ship, the USS SKYLARK {ASR 20), via UQC that depth was 400 feet and, at 0754R, that all future depths would be reported relative to test-depth: 1300-feet.

0845R: Main Coolant Pumps (MCPs} detected by SOSUS operating in FAST speed.

0909.0R; Continuous and erratic anomalous line frequency instability for two minutes as measured by a strong MCP rotational signal varying plus/minus 12 to 18 rpm.

0909.8R to 0911.3R: first failed attempt to deballast by blowing Main Ballast Tanks (MBTs}.

0911.0R: Strong MCP signal lost.

0913R: THRESHER via UQC "experiencing minor difficulties, have positive up angle, am attempting to blow, will keep you informed."

0913.6R to 0914.1R: SOSUS detection of second attempt to blow MBTs.

0917R: THRESHER via UQC: "900 North"

09:18:24R: SOSUS detection of hull collapse at a depth of 2400-feet.

There was no acoustic detection of MCPs operating in SLOW after the FAST speed signal was lost at 0911.0R nor was there any acoustic detection of main propulsion acoustic sources at any time. It is estimated such detections would have occurred had speeds above 12 knots been employed.

The following possibilities are advanced to provide the basis for further research into the cause of the loss of THRESHER over and above sea water flooding. There is no doubt a reactor scram occurred. The question is WHEN did it occur? If it occurred at 0909.0R, how did the Ship's Service Turbo-Generators (SSTGs} maintain Main Coolant Pumps (MCPs} in FAST for two minutes? This would have violated several operator procedural actions as well as probably exceeding the heat capacity of the steam generators. If not at 0909.0R, then why was there no evidence of the use of main propulsion to drive the ship up immediately after 0909.0R, negating the need to use Main Ballast Tank (MBT} blow at 0909.8R? If not at 0909.0R, then most definitely at 0911.0R when acoustic detection of the MCPs was lost. The frequency instability may provide the clue to what was happening. The SSTGs may have been operating in parallel or in an abnormal lineup, or propulsion may have been on the Emergency Propulsion Motor. In hindsight, these actions do not seem appropriate for the circumstance of being at test depth for the first time after the shipyard availability; however, testing of non nuclear propulsion equipment may have commenced, including, for example, the cycling of main sea water hull valves at test depth.

Simply put, USS THRESHER was lost because she was negatively buoyant. Apparently, Main Propulsion to drive the screw was not available to drive the ship towards the surface because of plant lineup or reactor scram procedural prohibition. The backup safety system of blowing MBTs was critically flawed. (attempts to deballast initiated at 0909.8R and 0913.6R (COI Finding of Fact 18) were unsuccessful because moisture in the flow-path from the high-pressure air flasks formed ice on strainers in the system valves: adiabatic cooling as confirmed during subsequent tests with the USS TINOSA (SSN 606).

(Adiabatic cooling is the process of reducing heat through a change in air pressure caused by volume expansion.)

The basic question is: Why was THRESHER negatively buoyant at test-depth?

SUGGESTIONS FOR FUTURE RESEARCH

Those who may, in the future, investigate the Joss of THRESHER should review the assessments provided by this document in six critical areas:

1. Assess the potential impact on safety-of-ship - especially during deep dives - of implementing procedures developed by personnel who had limited or no operational - at sea - experience.

2. Assess why design features that proved inadequate in the case of THRESHER were not recognized, and corrected before the disaster, such as the inability to effectively deballast at test-depth, and the potential consequences - relative to Joss of propulsion - of operating the Main Coolant Pumps (MCPs) in FAST (2-pole mode) during a deep-dive.

3. Assess why THRESHER could have been significantly heavy at test-depth if there was no flooding. (See last four paragraphs immediately above and ISSUES A, B and D below)

4. Calculate the average sink-rate and time required for a submarine with the displacement of a THRESHER/PERMIT Class hull - that lost propulsion while at speeds of less than five knots at a depth of 1300-feet - to reach 2400-feet if there had been no flooding and no compensation made for hull-compression at any depth greater than 100-feet. Compare those values with the acoustic-derived values for THRESHER of 120 feet-per minute and 9.5 minutes. Consider other factors such as adding sea water to sanitary tanks and possible leakage into the bilges from operation of sea water cooling systems.

5.   If THRESHER's main steam valves were closed immediately subsequent to the SSW reactor scram, assess how long decay-heat could have provided sufficient steam pressure to enable the Ship's Service Turbo Generators (SSTGs} - with action by the system speed governors - to generate near normal line-frequencies before the steam pressure dropped too low and the SSTG breakers tripped on under-frequency.

6.   Determine if the THRESHER deep-dive test-plan included cycling seawater hull valves and if that activity required shutting down one Ship's Service Turbo-Generator and disabling the main engine to the corresponding side - conditions that would have placed the propulsion plant at reduced readiness - in order to cycle the main condenser hull valves.

7.   Determine if THRESHER was scheduled to test the Emergency Propulsion Motor while at test-depth, a procedure that also would have reduced the readiness to respond to an emergency.

ISSUES AND REFERENCES

The following issues discuss information that has been derived since ADM Rickover made the above quoted assessment to Congress. Most significantly, in 2009, that the THRESHER pressure-hull collapsed at a depth of 2400-feet and, in 2016, the extreme rate of flooding that would have been associated with the COI conjectured rupture of a sea-connected pipe between two- and five-inches in diameter, values apparently never derived by the COI in 1963.

ISSUE A: NO FLOODING BEFORE COLLAPSE OF THRESHER's PRESSURE HULL AT GREAT DEPTH

Multiple, independent lines of evidence confirm there was no flooding prior to collapse of the THRESHER pressure-hull. Such flooding, conjectured by the COI to have been the initial and primary event responsible for the disaster, would have been a catastrophic event with the water-jet produced by the initial breaching of the pressure-hull or a pipe (OPINION 1a of the cited reference estimated the ruptured pipe to have been between two- and five-inches in diameter} expanding into the interior of the submarine with a velocity of about 1800 mph at THRESHER's depth of 1300-feet. Such an event would not have been reported by THRESHER to her escort ship, the USS SKYLARK at 0913R as (quote} experiencing minor difficulties (end quote}. Additionally, the conjectured flooding and the associated water-jet, upon impacting structures within the hull, would have generated extreme noise levels not only within the breached compartment but also in adjacent compartments, and at high levels throughout the submarine. Such noise levels would have made it essentially impossible for THRESHER to have communicated with SKYLARK. No such noise levels were evident during those communications nor were they detected by SOSUS. (Reference: Loss of the USS THRESHER: http://www.jag.navy.mil/ library/jagman investigations.htm http://www.jag.navy.mil/library/investigations/ USS%20THRESHER%20PT %201.pdf. 202.pdf, 203.pdf, 204.pdf

Another compelling reason for rejecting the Court Inquriy conjecture that flooding occurred at test-depth of 1300-feet (580 psi) is that water expanding into the relative vacuum (15 psi) within the THRESHER pressure-hull would have instantly atomized into a dense vapor (fog) upon impacting solid surfaces and/or vaporized in the low-pressure environment making it difficult to see within those spaces, yet immediately subsequent to telling SKYLARK at 0913R that she was (quote) experiencing minor difficulties (end quote), THRESHER transmitted (quote) Will keep you advised. (end quote). Neither of those transmissions are consistent with the disaster that flooding at test-depth would have represented.

(The following is reprised from another Chapter and Appendix A of this document) There is, in the public domain, a report by a former Commanding Officer (CO) of the USS SHARK (SSN 591) who claimed to have listened to a tape recording of UQC exchanges between THRESHER and SKYLARK that contained the following statement made by CO, THRESHER: (quote) Stand clear, emergency surfacing from test depth, flooding in the engine room. (end quote) Unfortunately for the accuracy of that memory and many other assertions made by the former CO, there was no tape recording to which he could have listened for- during Congressional hearings on the loss of THRESHER held on Thursday, 27 June 1963 - RADM John Maurer, Director, Submarine Warfare Division, in response to a question from Representative David Bates, NH stated: (quote) All of the ASRs are equipped with recorders now. This is since the (THRESHER) incident. At that time, they did not have recorders. (end quote) (Reference: Page 51 Congressional Record for 27 June 1963.)

A detailed rebuttal to all the misinformation provided by the former CO SHARK is provided by Appendix A. Source: http://www.iusscaa.org/articles/brucerule/ misinformation about the losswof thresher and the sosus detection thereof.htm

These assessments are confirmed by THRESHER Court of Inquiry Finding of Fact (FoF) 153, i.e., provides compelling support of the conclusion there was no flooding before collapse. FoF 153 states: (quote) That during the course of proceedings, a test demonstration for the Court of Inquiry was held in Drydock No. 2 at the Portsmouth Naval Shipyard. A stream of water was released to atmosphere at Thresher's test-depth pressure against a piece of electronic equipment. The stream produced tremendous force, spray, fog and noise (end quote), conditions -to repeat - that would not have been reported by THRESHER to SKYLARK as (quote) experiencing minor difficulties (end quote).

Russell Preble, CDR USN (ret), who was in Portsmouth, NH, in April 1963, and who actually observed that test, made the following statement: (quote) A memory that stands out in my mind was watching one of the Board of Inquiry's tests. An old SS radar console was placed on the floor of one of the empty dry docks and a high pressure stream of water was directed against the console. The noise was overwhelming. I remember thinking that nothing could be heard over the noise of the water smashing up against the radar casing and how at deep submergence no orders could be heard over the roar of water striking anything in its way. (end quote) (Reference: "USS Thresher, Lest We Forget", Burke Consortium, Inc, 2013, p. 5; file name: ThresherBooklet_printv2.pdf)

The above described THRESHER Court of Inquiry test confirmed that high-velocity water jets entering a submarine pressure-hull at great depth will generate extreme levels of acoustic energy (noise).

As of March 2007, the Office of Naval Intelligence still held acoustic detections of an event during which a water-jet (ram) with a velocity in excess of 2000 mph entered an otherwise intact submarine compartment at great depth. The acoustic energy produced during that event consisted of more than 100 individual narrowband resonances in the low - to mid-frequency spectrum. Those acoustic sources were detected as strong signals by a Sound Surveillance System (SOSUS) hydrophone array at a range in excess of 700 nautical miles.

The frequencies of such resonances are a function of the dimensions of objects directly or indirectly impacted by the high velocity water-jet. Such a water-jet essentially a water-ram- will excite not only the pressure-hull as it passes through a breach but, upon impacting internal structures, will act like a jackhammer.

Essentially, the submarine pressure-hull responds like an enormous bell being continuously struck by an equally outsized hydrostatically-driven clapper.

Impacted internal structures connected to the pressure-hull, bulkheads or decks respond like drumheads which resonate - as noted above - at frequencies that are a function of their dimensions - especially the thicknesses - of the component members of the excited structures.

The presence/absence of such resonances before the collapse of a submarine pressure-hull at great depth is an unambiguous indication of whether or not flooding occurred before collapse. No such signals were detected when THRESHER was lost only 30 nautical miles from the nearest SOSUS array.

And finally - immediately below - the most compelling reason of all for rejecting the COI conclusion that the reactor scram was the result of an electrical short circuit caused by the rupture of a sea-connected pipe while THRESHER was at test-depth (1300-feet).

The references cited below provide values for the rates at which flooding would have occurred aboard THRESHER had a pipe with a diameter between two- and five-inches actually ruptured at a depth of 1300-feet, as concluded by the COI. Those values are: (1) for a two-inch diameter pipe: 1800 gallons per minute (GPM), and (2), for a five-inch diameter pipe: 11,000 GPM.

In the four minutes that elapsed between loss of propulsion (the reactor scram) at 0909.0R - which was based on analysis of SOSUS data and which the Court of Inquiry attributed to the rupture of a sea-connected pipe - and the 0913R time of the (quote) experiencing minor difficulties (end quote) UQC transmission by THRESHER, we have the following values for flooding: (1) for a two-inch diameter pipe, flooding would have added 70,000 pounds, and (2), for a five-inch diameter pipe, flooding would have added 440,000 pounds. The Court of Inquiry apparently never made these calculations.

What makes the Court of Inquiry pipe-rupture-flooding assessment equally untenable are the volumes associated with those flooding rates: (1), for the two-inch pipe, a water volume of 965 cubic feet in four minutes, and (2), for the five-inch pipe, a water volume of 5,900 cubic feet in four minutes. Note: the volume of one US gallon is 0.134 cubic feet. Note: the weight of one galloon sea water is about 10 pounds. References:
(http://www.translatorscafe.com/cafe/EN/units-converter/pressure/38-59/psi foot sea water %2815%C2%BO%DO%A1%29/);
Convert PSI (sea pressure) and PSI (internal) and hole diameter (inches)
http://www.tlv.com/globai/TIIcalculator/water-flow-rate-through-orifice.html

SUMMARY ASSESSMENT OF ISSUE A:

For the multiple reasons discussed above, the THRESHER Court of Inquiry's conclusion that flooding occurred before collapse of the THRESHER pressure-hull and caused the reactor scram should be rejected. The proximate cause of the reactor scram remains unknown; however, it was NOT flooding.

ISSUE B: DERIVATION OF THRESHER PRESSURE-HULL COLLAPSE DEPTH

The THRESHER pressure-hull collapse depth calculation of 2400-feet - made for the first time in 2009 - is based on the empiric relationship that exists among three values: the depth at which collapse occurs, the volume of the collapsing structure, and the frequency of the bubble-pulse acoustic signal produced by the collapse: 3.4 Hz for THRESHER. (Reference: Page C4 of USS SCORPION (SSN 589) RESULTS OF NOL DATA ANALYSIS (U) (NOL Ltr 69-160 of 29 January 1970), Robert Price and Ermine Christian).

As discussed in an earlier section of this assessment, the calculated collapse depth of 2400-feet at 09:18:24R also is consistent with the conclusion that the phrase "900 North" transmitted by THRESHER to SKYLARK at 0917R via UQC was an indirect reference to test-depth, as required for security reasons, i.e., THRESHER was 900 feet below test-depth or at 2200-feet about 90 seconds before collapse of the pressure-hull 200 feet deeper.

Survival of the THRESHER pressure-hull and all sea-connected systems to a depth 450-feet greater than the calculated collapse depth of 1950-feet (test-depth plus 50%) exculpates all Portsmouth Naval Shipyard personnel of any complicity in the loss of THRESHER. Indeed, "they built better than they knew."

A corollary of the depth derivation and measurement of the bubble-pulse frequency (BPF) is determination of the energy release - expressed in pounds of TNT- required to produce the observed BPF at the derived depth. In the case of THRESHER, the value was 22,500 pounds of TNT, produced by the nearly instantaneous conversion of potential energy (1070 psi sea pressure) to kinetic energy, the motion of the water-ram which entered the THRESHER pressure-hull with a velocity of about 2600 mph (3800 feet-per-second) at the collapse depth of 2400-feet.

THRESHER was destroyed (fragmented) in about 0.047 seconds (112Qth of a second), the assessed duration of the compression phase of the collapse event. That value is less than the combined retinal and cognitive integration times (0.08-0.10 seconds) of those aboard, i.e., they were not aware of the event; it occurred too fast to be apprehended. (See Chapter 2).

ISSUE C: DERIVATION OF AND EXPLANATION FOR THRESHER's AVERAGE SINK-RATE OF 120 FEET A MINUTE

THRESHER was at or near test-depth (1300-feet) at 0909.0R at which time propulsion was lost. THRESHER's pressure-hull collapsed at 09:18:24R at a depth of 2400-feet.

THRESHER's depth increased 1100-feet (1300 to 2400) in 9.5 minutes (0909.0R-09:18:24R) for an average sink-rate of about 120-feet a minute (ft/min). That rate would have accelerated over time because of the effects of hull-compression with depth, e.g., constant weight (no flooding) with decreasing displacement.

The 120 ft/min average value for THRESHER compares with a 52 ft/min average for the USS SCORPION which sank in 21 mins and 50 sees from an estimated transit depth not greater than 400-feet at the time of the internally destructive battery explosion (18:20:44Z, 22 May 1968) to collapse at a depth of 1530-feet at 18:42:34Z. The calculated atmospheric over-pressure created by the battery explosion was 150-200 psi at the site of the event, seven to 10 times the fatal value; hence, it is improbable SCORPION's sink-rate was slowed by actions of the crew who were either killed or functionally incapacitated by the battery event. ((Chapter SIX of 'Why The USS SCORPION (SSN-589) Was Lost, ISBN 978-1-60888-120-8, Nimble Books, 31 October 2011)) This book was reviewed/ commented upon by (1), Letter to the Editor Fall 2011 Issue of THE SUBMARINE REVIEW, pp 149-150), (2), The Loss of SCORPION, a Book Review, Winter 2012 Issue of THE SUBMARINE REVIEW, pp 151-152), and (3), Letter to the Editor Summer 2012 Issue of THE SUBMARINE REVIEW, pp 141)

It is concluded THRESHER sank at an average of 120 ft/min subsequent to loss of propulsion at test-depth because the submarine was heavy overall by an estimated 12,000 pounds and unable to deballast, and not because of flooding. The heavy overall condition is attributed to failure to compensate for hull compression with increases in depth below 100-feet.

As implausible - and unacceptable to some - as this explanation may be, the elimination of flooding as a possibility (Issue A above) leaves no other explanation for the documented average THRESHER sink-rate of 120 ft/min.

Those who question this explanation of the documented sink-rate should perform the calculations suggested by (4) under "SUGGESTIONS FOR FUTURE RESEARCH" above.

The significantly lower average sink-rate (52ft/min)- discussed above- indicates SCORPION was closer to being neutrally buoyant than was THRESHER when propulsion was lost.

ISSUE D: ACOUSTIC DETECTIONS OF THRESHER's MAIN COOLANT PUMPS AND THE TIME OF THE REACTOR SCRAM (SHUT-DOWN).

While passing a depth of 1000 feet during the scheduled 10 April 1963 deep-dive to test-depth (1300-feet), rotational-rates of THRESHER's Main Coolant Pumps (MCPs) were initially detected acoustically at 0845R in FAST (2-pole mode). Identification of that detection as an MCP source was based on the involved narrowband frequencies and the coincident detection of an associated acoustic source at a fixed ratio of 0.485:1 to the MCP rotational rates, a value unique to S5W reactor system MCPs. That detection - and all subsequent detections of MCP activity and the two unsuccessful attempts to deballast (0909.8R-0911.3R and 0913.5R-0914.1R)- were made at a range of 30 nautical miles by SOSUS hydrophone array FOX which terminated at HMCS Shelburne, Nova Scotia. Note: the durations of those attempted deballasting events represent the periods during which pressure-induced oscillations of any escaped air produced detectable signals, NOT the functioning duration of the attempt to deballast. Source: http://www.jag.navy.mil/library/investigations/USS%20THRESHER %20PT%201.pdf

The line-frequency of the non-vital electrical buses that powered the MCPs in FAST (2-pole mode) was established by correcting the frequency of the MCP rotational-rates for the 2.5 percent slip-rate of the MCP drive-motors. The implied non-vital bus line-frequency and stability were normal - until 0909.0R- based on comparisons with analyses by the author of several thousand hours of previous SOSUS detections of S5W SSTG systems- including THRESHER from pre overhaul detections - published by Commander Oceanographic System, Atlantic on 1 April 1963 as THE US NUCLEAR SUBMARINE ACOUSTIC DATA HANDBOOK.".

The results of analyses of the HMCS Shelburne acoustic data were provided by the author to the THRESHER COI on 18 April 1963 and are summarized in Part I of the U.S. Navy Judge Advocate General's Report of the loss of the USS THRESHER available at http://www.jag.navy.mil/library/jagman investigations.htm

At 0909.0R, the MCP rotational rates- still in FAST- became unstable, varying randomly plus/minus 12-18 rpm until 0911.0R when the signal was abruptly lost while still in FAST. As of March 2007, the Office of Naval Intelligence still held a photocopy of the original graphic paper display (LOFARgram) upon which this 1963 analysis was based. There were no magnetic tape recordings of any SOSUS detection of the THRESHER event, only paper data displays. (See Appendix A.) The original SOSUS lofargrams were destroyed by Commander, Oceanographic System, Atlantic on 22 May 1968 because the event was more than five years old. By late May 1968, it was determined SCORPION was lost on the same day as the THRESHER acoustic data was destroyed: 22 May.

SUMMARY ASSESSMENT OF ISSUE D

Because of the highly anomalous instability of the MCP acoustic signal - which was a reflection of instability of the same magnitude in the line-frequency of the non-vital buses powering the MCPs which began at 0909.0R- and initiation of the first failed attempt to deballast at 0909.8R- it is assessed the reactor scram occurred at 0909.0R with the MCPs in FAST, two minutes before the Court of Inquiry's assessed time of 0911.0R.

Had THRESHER retained a propulsion capability after 0909.0R, the attempt to deballast initiated about 48 seconds later- at 0909.8R- should not have been necessary; THRESHER could have used propulsion to drive to the surface, an evolution that should have been detected by the HMCS Shelburne SOSUS array had a speed greater than about 12 knots been employed. No such detection occurred. The rapid response: an attempt to deballast only 48 seconds atter loss of propulsion suggests it was almost immediately evident to THRESHER that depth was increasing, a circumstance that supports the conclusion THRESHER was seriously heavy (negatively buoyant) at test-depth.

Confirmation that the reactor scram with the resulting loss of propulsion occurred before 0909.8R is a critical assessment because that assessment, in turn, confirms flooding did not cause the scram- contrary to the COI conclusion - because, at 0913R, THRESHER transmitted to SKYLARK that she was (quote) experiencing minor difficulties (end quote) when, as previously discussed, the COI's own test demonstrated flooding at test-depth would have been a catastrophic event that would have made any communications with SKYLARK essentially impossible

The THRESHER Court of Inquiry had this information in 1963 but still attributed the disaster to flooding which caused the reactor scram: loss of propulsion.

ISSUE E: AN EXPLANATION OF THE REPORTED CONDITION OF THE THRESHER WRECKAGE: IN SIX MAJOR SECTIONS.

Imagery is reported to indicate the THRESHER wreckage is in six major sections. The probable temporal dynamics of collapse events provide an explanation for that condition.

The estimated velocity of the water-ram which entered the THRESHER pressure hull at the collapse depth of 2400-feet was 2600 mph or about 4-feet per millisecond (0.001s). At that velocity, the ram would have traversed the maximum internal diameter of the pressure-hull in about 0.008s. Note; however, that the initial breach also would have created a shock-wave that propagated through the entire pressure-hull at the velocity of the speed of sound in steel: about 20,000 feet per-second or 20-feet per millisecond, five times the velocity of the water ram.

That shock-wave, acting on a structure already stressed to the point of collapse throughout its entire length, probably triggered additional structural failures before flooding from the initial breach reached those failure points. Those additional failures probably tore the pressure-hull longitudinally - as was the case with the Israeli submarine DAKAR - and vertically thus separating the THRESHER pressure-hull as imaged. (See Appendix C).

This is an important assessment because it explains why apparent (imaged) multiple points of failure of a collapsed submarine pressure-hull can, in fact, be the result of a single point of failure.

Note again that the entire THRESHER pressure-hull was destroyed (collapsed) in 47 milliseconds, about half the minimum time required for human cognitive perception of such an event. (See Chapter 2)

Also note that the dynamic forces associated with the collapse of a submarine pressure-hull at great depth are sufficient to cancel all pre existing directions of motion even in the unlikely circumstance that collapse occurs at high speed. Wreckage will sink vertically from the point of collapse at speeds of 10-13 knots. Such cancellation did not occur with either THRESHER or SCORPION because they had no velocity component at the times of collapse other than vertical at about two- and one-knot, respectively.

ISSUE F: SECURITY ISSUES ASSOCIATED WITH DISCUSSION OF THE LOSS OF THE USS THRESHER

The author's letter of 10 April 2013 to RADM Richard P. Breckenridge - which deals with the classification of information related to the loss of THRESHER - is available in full at
http://www.iusscaa.org/articles/brucerule/letter_to_the_deputy_cno.htm.

Section VI of that letter states: (quote) Reference (c) (below), published in the Federal Register on 5 January 2010, provides guidance concerning the long-term classification of documents with reference to content. Specifically, reference (c) defines (quote) damage to the national security (as) harm to the national defense or foreign relations of the United States from unauthorized disclosure of information, to include the sensitivity, value, and utility of that information. (end quote)

Reference (d) establishes the criteria for classification of information as material the disclosure of which would damage the national security and requires the original classification authority to identify or describe the damage, I.e, information cannot be classified by fiat.

This is the standard against which any security concerns about the timeline of events that occurred onboard the USS THRESHER on 10April1963 (derived from acoustic data) must be validated. Part 3 of reference (e) also applies to this classification/release issue.

In summary, any contention that conclusions in this document about the loss of the USS THRESHER derived from acoustic data are classified must meet the requirements for classification established by references (c), (d) and (e), and also must acknowledge information that may be in question is available in the public domain as Finding of Fact 153 and/or the OPINIONs of reference (a) or can be derived from that information, e.g., MCPs operating speeds (modes): FAST and SLOW.

Reference (h) is one of many internet sites that provide information germane to that specific subject area, e.g., (quote) Coolant pump switch. 6 pumps, each with fast and slow speeds. Only used 4 at a time underway.... they're running 2 slow-2 slow (2 slow speed pumps port, and another 2 starboard. (end quote)

Reference (i) cannot be applied to the contents of this document because this document does not provide information on (quote) overside noise (by identifying frequencies, radiated noise levels, structures or specific bandwidths of that noise), platform noise or sonar self-noise signatures (end quote) beyond that already provided by reference (a) and in the public domain.

(a) Loss of the USS THRESHER: http://www.jag.nayy.milllibrary/jagman investigations.htm http://www.jag.nayy.milllibrarv/investigations/ USS%20THRESHER%20PT
%201.pdf, 202.pdf, 203.pdf, 204.pdf
(c) Administration of Barack H. Obama, memorandum of 29 Dec 2009 Implementation of Executive Order: Classified National Security Information
(d) Presidential Executive Order 12958 of 17 April 1995
(e) Executive Order 13526 of 29 December 2009
(h) http://www.flickr.com/photos/oneillparker/3224878652/
(i) OPNAVINST 5513.5C: Security Classification Guide 05-37

CHAPTER 2

THRESHER and SCORPION Collapse Events

Occurred Too Fast to be Perceived by Those Aboard

Monograph of 24 August 2016

Subj: THRESHER and SCORPION Collapse Events Occurred Too Fast to be Perceived by Those Aboard

SUMMARY

This article provides data from the 2016 Olympics (5) to establish that the implosive collapse of the THRESHER and SCORPION pressure-hulls at great depth occurred too fast to be cognitively recognized by those aboard. There was no sequential flooding of individual compartments on a perceptible time scale.

DISCUSSION: TEMPORAL CHARACTERISTICS OF COLLAPSE EVENTS

Invalidation of the assumption that the initial compression and expansion (rebound) phases of the collapse of a submarine pressure-hull at great depth are symmetrical (of equal duration), and measurement of the acoustic signal (bubble pulse) created by the collapse of the SCORPION pressure-hull indicate THRESHER and SCORPION collapsed (complete destruction: fragmentation/compression) in not more than about one-sixth of the reciprocal of their respective bubble-pulse frequencies of 3.4 Hz and 4.46 Hz or in 0.047 seconds and 0.037 seconds, respectively. (See Chapter 3)

Temporal asymmetry - repeat, asymmetry - exists between the compression and expansion phases of submarine pressure-hull collapse events because the duration of the collapse phase is truncated by the collapse phase pressure wave encountering the compacting mass of the hull and internal structures whereas the expansion (rebound) phase terminates less abruptly when the falling pressure and momentum of that expanding wave is overcome by the ambient pressure at the collapse depth. (See Appendix D)

During the 0.037s (37 millisecond) duration of the compression phase of the SCORPION collapse event, two after compartments were symmetrically "telescoped" (one within the other) a distance of about 50-feet. Those time and distance values require an average velocity for the forward moving hull sections of about 900 mph, three times a previously estimated value which was based on the incorrect assumption that the durations of the compression and expansion phases were equal. The velocity of the water-ram that provided this compressive force was 2000 mph.

It was this enormous axially-aligned forward vector - opposed (primarily) by inertial forces (a body at rest tends to stay at rest) acting on both the shaft and the propeller, and (secondarily) by the resistance of the water acting on the effective blade area of the propeller that tore the shaft - with the propeller still attached - from the thrust block and out of the submarine where it fell separately to the bottom to be imaged near the telescoped after hull sections by TRIESTE.

This assessment resolves the long-standing question: was loss of the propeller shaft the cause or the result of the loss of the USS SCORPION? DISCUSSION: MINIMUM HUMAN REACTION TIMES TO EXTERNAL STIMULI

The most accurate assessments of the minimum (quickest) human reaction time

(actual motion) to external stimuli-such as the failure of a submarine pressure hull - is provided by electronic measurement - accurate to the millisecond (ms) - of the elapsed time between the firing of the starting-gun at Olympic 100m sprint event and the increase in foot-pressure on the "pedals" of a sprinter's starting blocks measured by sensors in the blocks. Those sensors are activated when the runner reacts to the gun and begins to drive out of the blocks. The transducer that detects the gun-signal for automated comparison with the block-signal is usually strapped to the gun to eliminate sound travel-time of the signal in air to a sensor remote from the gun. Additionally, the gun-signal is transmitted electronically to a speaker immediately behind each runner for all races run in lanes which may locate runners in lane eight significantly distant from those runners in lane one. (This apparently extraneous information is provided to permit the reader to quantify the potential errors in human reaction times as measured at the 2016 Olympics during the trials, semi-finals and finals of the 100m sprint event.)

Such measurement systems are used by the IAAF (International Association of Athletic Federations) to identify reaction times below the accepted minimum value possible for any athlete: 0.11 seconds (110 ms). Detection of reaction times of 0.10 seconds or less indicate a "false start" and require disqualification of the runner.

For the 100m finals at the 2016 Olympics, the reaction times for the eight finalists are listed below in the order of finish. The range of reaction times for those runners during preliminary heats, quarterfinal and semifinal events are provided in parens. (All values in seconds.)

1. Usian Bolt: 0.155 (0.146-0.156) '
2. Justin Gatlin: 0.152 (0.151- 0.160)
3. Andre De Grasse: 0.141 (0.130- 0.148)
4. Yohan Blake: 0.145 (0.147- 0.154)
5. Akani Simbine: 0.128 (0.124- 0.144)

6. Ben Youssef Meite: 0.156 (0.142- 0.145)
7. Jimmy Vicaut: 0.140 (0.131- 0.164)
8. Trayvon Bromell: 0.135 (0.128-0.165)

The average of all these times is 0.145 or 145 ms.

CONCLUSIONS

The response (reaction) times of those eight specially-trained and highly conditioned athletes significantly exceed the time during which both THRESHER and SCORPION pressure-hulls were completely destroyed, i.e., reached the point of maximum fragmentation/compression. There was no sequential flooding of individual internal compartments on a time-scale perceptible to those aboard. Instantaneously fatal injuries occurred during periods significantly less than 0.047 seconds for THRESHER and 0.037 seconds for SCORPION, respectively, one 20th of a second and one 27th of a second. (See Chapter 3)

Footnote (6), "The Timing of the Cognitive Cycle," states:"••.initial phase of perception (stimulus recognition) occurs 80-100 ms from stimulus onset under optimal conditions."

The assessments that those aboard SCORPION and THRESHER died in less than 37-47 ms (1/27th and 1/20th of a second, respectively) and that cognitive recognition of an external stimuli requires 80-100 ms confirm that no one aboard THRESHER or SCORPION was aware of those collapse events; they occurred too fast to be apprehended.

It is concluded those lost aboard THRESHER and SCORPION did not drown or otherwise suffer physical pain when collapse occurred. They simply did not know the events occurred.

Footnotes:

(1) http://wwwjag.navy.mil/librazy/jarmum investi"ations.htm (Part one of the U.S. Navy Judge Advocate General's Report of the Joss of the USS THRESHER)
(2) Why The USS SCORPION (SSN-589) Was Lost." Nimble Books LLC 2011, ISBN 978-1-60888-120-8
(3)   ProjectAZORIAN, The CIA and the Raising of the K-129. Norman Polmar and Michael White, Naval Institute Press, ISBN 978-1-59114-690-2, pp 162-167
(4)   THE SUBMARINE REVIEW, Spring 2012, "Russian SSBNs -ADead Man Launch Capability?"
(5)   https://en.wikipedia.orfVwiki/Athletics at the 2016 Summer Olympics- Men %o27s_100_metres
(6)   http://www.ncbi.nlm.nih.gov/pmc/articles/PMC3081809/

CHAPTER 3

Distinguishing Acoustic Detections of Explosions

From Implosions, a Critical Analysis Capability

Monograph of 4 October 2016

Subj: Distinguishing Acoustic Detections of Explosions from Implosions, a Critical Analysis Capability

BACKGROUND

If underwater explosions or implosions do not vent to the surface, they produce cycles of expansion and compression of the area of affected pressure - basically a vacuum bubble - created by the involved energy release. The oscillations (movement) of the water displaced by both types of events generate high levels of acoustic energy that can be detected at thousands of nautical miles unless bathymetrically occluded. (See Appendix D)

The ability to distinguish acoustic detections of explosions from implosions can provide critically important information not available from any other source. In the case of the loss of the USS SCORPION (SSN 589) on 22 May 1968, that analysis capability would have prevented the Navy's SCORPION Court of Inquiry from erroneously concluding SCORPION was lost because of "the explosion of a large charge weight external to the pressure-hull." That assessment was generatively responsible not only for the basic misapprehension of why the disaster occurred but also for subsequent conspiracy theories that SCORPION was sunk by a Soviet torpedo. (See Appendix B.)

(SCORPION was lost because of an explosion of hydrogen out-gassed by the main battery. That explosion - which was contained within the pressure-hull - disabled and/or killed the crew, who were unable to prevent SCORPION from sinking to a depth of 1530-feet (680 psi) where the pressure-hull imploded with an energy release equal to the explosion of 13,200 lbs of TNT at that depth.)

DISCUSSIONS

Hot gases produced by an underwater explosion are contained within a bubble which rapidly expands. As the bubble expands, the pressure inside decreases. The momentum of the displaced water continues the expansion of the bubble beyond the point at which the internal pressure falls below the external (sea) pressure. When this pressure-difference becomes sufficient to overcome the momentum, the bubble contracts, compressing the gas within until its pressure is sufficient to halt the motion of the water, whereupon the cycle repeats, each time with diminished amplitude and duration because of the loss of energy due to friction. The oscillating bubble generates a series of pressure pulses known as "bubble pulses" which are characteristics of deep underwater explosions. (1)

Unlike the expansion phase of the cycle of the explosion-generated bubble, the duration of the contraction phase is halted abruptly when the basically non compressible water "meets" at the "focal point" of the event: the site of the explosion; however, each phase "travels" the same distance and may have approximately the same duration. Note: extremely high time-resolution analyses of underwater explosive events are needed to refine this assessment.

Different phase duration relationship exist for implosions. The initial phase is the contraction of the "bubble" which is essentially the air contained within the imploding object - in the context of this discussion - the collapse of a submarine pressure-hull. When that compression reaches the maximum value, the bubble expands until - as was the case discussed above for the expansion phase of an explosive event, it is overcome by ambient sea-pressure. Therefore, the expansion-compression phase relationship of a implosion should differ significantly from an explosive event, e.g., the phase relationship of the implosion is compression short, expansion long while the explosive event phases may be much closer to the same duration.

Extremely accurate measurements of the durations of these phases - and the sequence in which they occur -should permit identification of the source of an acoustic event, i.e., distinguish hydroacoustically detected explosions from implosions. Appendix C provides additional information on collapse events which support these assessments.

DATA MEASUREMENTS

Only one acoustic event analyzed in the required temporal resolution was available to the writer for evaluation of the above discussed assessments: the SCORPION pressure-hull collapse event shown as the figure in Chapter 4 of reference (2). That display has an effective time-resolution of 0.003 seconds ((three milliseconds (ms)). Note: as of March 2007, the Office of Naval Intelligence still retained recordings of other collapse events from the temporal durations of the compression and expansion phases of submarine pressure-hull collapse events can be determined.

The temporal characteristics of the first collapse-expansion cycle created by the collapse of the SCORPION pressure-hull -as detected at a range of 821 nautical miles - had a duration of 0.224 seconds. The displayed changes in signal level during that period are consistent with the following assessment: the collapse phase of the event had a duration of about 37 milliseconds (ms) (1/27th of a second) while the expansion phase had a duration of about 187 ms (1/Sth of a second); hence, the **asymmetry** between the durations of the expansion and compression phases of a submarine pressure-hull collapse event may be a great as five-to-one, a value consistent with the travel-distance of the compression phase: less than half the diameter of the pressure-hull. Additionally, the noise level generated during the expansion phase of the SCORPION event was significantly higher than during the collapse phase. (See Appendix D)

If dissimilar relative temporal and amplitude characteristics can be identified for signals known to have been of explosive origin, these differences can be used to reliably identify acoustic detections of such events as either explosions or implosions.

COMMENT

There were no recordings of the collapse of the THRESHER pressure-hull. The most-accurate THRESHER bubble-pulse frequency of 3.4 Hz was derived from analysis of paper displays (AN-FQQ-1M vernier LOFARgrams} from the Antigua SOSUS station at a detection range of 1,300 nautical miles. That frequency value (3.4 Hz} indicated the THRESHER pressure-hull collapsed at a depth of 2400- feet with an energy release equal to the explosion of 22,500 lbs of TNT at that depth. If the same ratio of compression duration to expansion duration existed for THRESHER as for SCORPION, the THRESHER pressure-hull collapsed - was completely destroyed - in about 47ms (1/20th of a second). Sea pressure at the THRESHER collapse depth was 1070 psi.

CONCLUSION

This assessment is yet another example of the axiom: the more carefully you measure something, the more you find out about related subjects: in this case, measurement in the time domain to an accuracy of several milliseconds. The resulting loss of frequency resolution from such signal processing is of no consequence because the frequency of the bubble-pulse can be derived with extreme accuracy as the reciprocal of the duration of the event: 4.46 Hz for SCORPION as shown by the above discussed figure.

ANCILLARY ISSUE

During the SCORPION Court of Inquiry hearings, the Court was misinformed by an assessment - which they fully accepted - that the bubble pulse acoustic signal created by the collapse of a submarine pressure-hull might not be detectable because it could be "swallowed" within the pressure-hull and thus not be detected by acoustic sensors (hydrophones} remote from the location of the event.

As discussed by Appendix B, that assessment is refuted by the temporal dynamics of submarine collapse events: the pressure-hull is destroyed during the collapse phase; hence, there is no structure left intact that could contain ("swallow") the signal as it expands from the point of maximum compression.

Had the SCORPION Court of Inquiry examined the findings of the THRESHER Court of Inquiry, they would have known that submarine pressure-hull collapse event signals propagate to extreme ranges in the open ocean. They would NOT have accepted John Craven's "swallowing" conjecture which was the basis for their erroneous conclusion that the acoustic event associated with the loss of SCORPION was produced by the "explosion of a large charge weight external to the pressure-hull,' i.e., they concluded that acoustic detection of the event meant it could not have been collapse of the SCORPION pressure-hull because such events are "swallowed," and; hence, undetectable. (See Appendix B.)

Refined measurement of the acoustic data in 2008 indicated the frequency of the SCORPION pressure-hull collapse signal (the bubble-pulse) was 4.46 Hz.

SOURCES

(1) https://books.google.com/books?
id=acOaAgAAQBAJ&pg=PT135&1pg=PT135&dq=bubble+pulse+noise&source=b
l&ots=YPucq9LGsU&sig=UUuFie77Vs8hHVfoGNoFIFOrvCo&hl=en&sa=X&ved=
OahUKEwiZ1d3u-7_PAhWEPiYKHdMJDH4Q6AEIIzAB#v=onepage&q=bubble
%20pulse%20noise&f=false

(2) "WHY THE USS SCORPION WAS LOST; DEATH OF A SUBMARINE IN THE NORTH ATLANTIC." Nimble Books LLC, ISBN 978-1-60888-120-8, 31 Oct 2011

APPENDIX A

Misinformation in the Public Domain About the Loss of THRESHER

Monograph of 1 July 2013

Subj: Misinformation in the Public Domain About the Loss of THRESHER

PREFACE

Sections of this monograph - originally written as a stand-alone document - have been reprised in earlier chapters of this book to provide useful background information.

DISCUSSIONS

The Prologue to the THRESHER BOOKLET {http://www.bonefishbase.omt\m content/ uploads/2011110/Thresher-Booklet.pdf} states (quote) putting together the history of the development of the SUBSAFE program as it was established and evolved by collecting stories, recollections of events, and related documents from those that participated would be worthwhile. (end quote)

Statements in the THRESHER BOOKLET by CAPT Zeb Alford (1925-2009) are provided below in full. Those statements of special interest are foot-noted (1) through (8) with references to Navy Judge Advocate General THRESHER Court of Inquiry documents that provide information relavent to those statements.

If the reader finds difficulty accessing the websites provided below, go to the Navy JAG site: http://www.jag.navy.miVlibrruy/jagman investigations.htm, scroll down the date and event columns to 1963fTHRESHER, then click on each of the four documents listed as Parts I through IV.

It is very difficult to understand how CAPT Alford could have been as misinformed as he was but regardless of why he was so misinformed, his statements are an example of the erroneous assessments extant in the public domain about the loss of the USS THRESHER. The author went to the publisher of the THRESHER BOOKLET for comment but receive no response.

CAPT Zeb Alford statements in the THRESHER BOOKLET (quoted in full as follows from page 6):

I was CO of the USS SHARK at that time (of the loss of THRESHER) and on a special op. I couldn't believe the message we received.

The CO of THRESHER, Wes Harvey, was a close friend and one of the most qualified nuclear engineers I ever had the honor to serve with. We put the USS

TULLIBEE nuclear prototype and USS TULLIBEE, our first nuclear SSK, in commission. Wes was the engineer for both and I was XO.

In November 1963 ADM Rickover had me ordered to the Pentagon to OP 31. VADM Dennis Wilkerson was my boss there. The task he assigned me, among others, was to get together all the information pertinent to the loss of the THRESHER, and write the presentation to Congress by VADM Red Ramage (OP 03) concerning the case. I was also assigned as project manager for the SUBSAFE program for CNO. My saddest memory was listening to the tapes of the underwater phone conversations between Wes and the submarine rescue vessel (1), which was his escort for his sea trials, after a major overhaul at Portsmouth Naval Shipyard. Wes had relieved him as CO while the sub was in the shipyard.. The first conversation that I remember well was Wes telling the sub rescue vessel to "stand clear, emergency surfacing from test depth, flooding in the engine room." (2)

His voice was calm and easily recognized. I could hear the air blow start and the screw speeding up. In less than a minute, the emergency blow trailed off and the screw started slowing down. (3) Wes's last report was "attempting to blow." Wes knew and I knew that there were no orders that started with "attempting." His voice was still calm even though he knew by then his sub was lost. I believe to this day that he was telling us something was wrong with the air blow system. Even someone as good an engineer as Wes couldn't figure out why the air blow stopped. The next thing on the tape some minutes later was the collapse of the first bulkhead, followed shortly after with the others collapsing. (4) Calculations later estimated the sub reached 300-400 feet depth before the flooding stopped her ascent. (5) Six weeks later when she was located, the bow was buried about thirty feet deep. (6) Calculations show she was going over 100 knots when she bottomed. (7) The front half of the sub was vertical and the sub broke in two at the reactor compartment. (8) I could read the name of the next to last reactor watch officer on the log sheet on the bottom of the ocean from the hundreds of pictures taken.

ZEB ALFORD

FOOTNOTES:

(1) During Congressional hearings on the loss of THRESHER held on Thursday, 27 June 1963, RADM John Maurer, Director, Submarine Warfare Division, in response to a question from Representative David Bates, NH, stated: (quote) All of the ASRs are equipped with recorders now. This is since the (THRESHER) incident. At that time, they did not have recorders. (end quote) Page 51 Congressional Record for 27 June 1963.

Because the USS SKYLARK (ASR-20) did not have the capability to record the underwater communications with THRESHER, the content of those communications was established by the Court of Inquiry through extensive, direct examination of those aboard SKYLARK who were present when the communications occurred. The transcript of that direct examination is provided by htto:/lwww.jag.navy.mil/library/investigations/USS%20THRESHER%20PT%203.pdf

(2) http://www.jag.navy.milllibrary/investigations/USS%20THRESHER%20PT%201.pdf. THRESHER Court of Inquiry Court of Inquiry Fact 16 provides the agreed (among those onboard the SKYLARK) content of an underwater telephone (UQC) transmission by THRESHER at 0913 on 10 April 1963 to have been: (quote) Experiencing minor difficulties. Have positive up angle. Am attempting to blow. Will keep you informed. (end quote). No THRESHER Court of Inquiry document discusses the (quote) stand clear, emergency surfacing from test depth, flooding in the engine room (end quote) transmission attributed to THRESHER by CAPT Alford.

(3) There is no discussion in any THRESHER Court of Inquiry document of the THRESHER (quote) screw speeding up (end quote) or subsequently (quote) slowing down. (end quote) Additionally, there was no Sound Surveillance System (SOSUS) acoustic detection of THRESHER main propulsion activity nor was there any detection of a Doppler component that could have been produced by the such activity. As of March 2007, the Office of Naval Intelligence (ONI) still held a photo copy of the original SOSUS time versus frequency paper display (LOFARgram) upon which this assessment is based. There were no SOSUS tape recordings of the period during which THRESHER was lost, only the paper displays.

(4) From a human perception standpoint (had there been a tape recording), there would have been only one audible collapse event. The acoustic (LOFARgram) data ONI still held in March 2007 confirms the duration of the collapse event, which occurred at a subsequently revised time of 09:18:24R, was the reciprocal of the bubble-pulse frequency or about one-tenth of a second corrected for the asymmetry between the compression and expansion phases of the collapse event bubble-pulse or 0.047 seconds, the period during which the THRESHER pressure-hull and all internal compartments were destroyed and the pressure-hull fragmented into sections that sank independently from the collapse depth of 2400 feet at an estimated speed of about 12 knots. Additionally, as discussed above. SKYLARK had no record capability. Much of the acoustic information derived from analysis of the LOFARgram displays by the author, and provided to the THRESHER Court Inquiry in closed testimony on 18 April 1963, is contained in Court of Inquiry OPINIONS in http://www.jag.navy.milllibrary/investigations/USS%20THRESHER%20PT%202.pdf

(5) There is no discussion in any Court of Inquiry document of calculations that indicated THRESHER (quote) reached a depth of 300-400 feet before the flooding stopped her ascent. (end quote)

(6) There is no discussion in any Court of Inquiry document that the THRESHER (quote) bow was buried thirty feet deep. (end quote). Such an impact would have been detected by SOSUS as seismic and/or acoustic energy at the event range of 30 nautical miles from the nearest hydrophone array. No such detection occurred. Additionally, during testimony before the Court of Inquiry, SKYLARK personnel testified they heard nothing over the UQC subsequent to the collapse of the THRESHER pressure-hull. (Source: http://www.jag.navy.mil/library/ investigations/USS%20THRESHER%20PT %203.pdf-Part III.

(7) Appendix A to Naval Ordnance laboratory letter serial 69-160 of 20 January 1970 states the average sink-rate of the fully-flooded USS STERLET (SS-392) hulk was 12.9 knots in 10,700 feet of water. Acoustic data provided by the author to ONI in October 2009 indicates the average sink-rate of the USS SCORPION (SSN-589) hull sections was less than 28 knots in 11,100 feet of water. Open source data indicates the intact MIKE Class Soviet nuclear submarine, fully flooded with the exception of the first compartment, had an average sink-rate of 10-12 knots in 5,528 feet of water. The conclusion that THRESHER, which was destroyed when the pressure-hull collapsed, impacted the bottom at a speed of (quote) over 100 knots (end quote) would, if still intact and in a vertical bow-down position, have required more than half a million shaft horsepower to reach a terminal velocity of 100 knots. Note: no WWII depth charge, even those designed to be as hydrodynamically efficient as possible, had sink-rates in excess of 50 f/s (30 knots).

Also note: the propulsive power requirements of a given submerged submarine of a given displacement vary as a cube of the speed. (Concepts in Submarine Design; Roy Burcher and Louis J. Rydill, Oct 27, 1995) Given, for the sake of this discussion, that THRESHER was still intact (not in six major sections) and had achieved a sink-rate of 30 knots in a bow-down position, to achieve a bottom impact speed of 100 knots (about 3.5 times her maximum speed which required 15,000 shaft horsepower), we have 3.5 cubed (42.9) times 15,000 or about 650,000 shaft horsepower to achieve 100 knots, and CAPT Alford says "over 100 knots."

(For those who remember the statement in "BLIND MAN'S BLUFF" that the GOLF-II Class Soviet ballistic missile submarine (SSB) K-129 impacted the bottom at 200 knots - attributed to an unidentified Navy report - which is approximately 14 times greater than the 14 knots the K-129 could achieve submerged with 5,400 horsepower (hp), we have the following calculations: 14 cubed is 2744 which, times 5,400 hp, equals 14,800,000 shaft hp for the K-129 to achieve 200 knots. At such speeds, the outer, "light" hull and the sail would have been carried away. Images of the K-129 wreckage available in "PROJECT AZORIAN, THE CIA AND THE RAISING OF THE K-129" by Norman Polmar and Michael White indicate this was not the case: masts in the sail were still in the deployed (raised) position without evident damage.

(8) There is no discussion in any Court of Inquiry document that indicates (quote) The front half of the sub was vertical... (end quote). Imagery of the THRESHER site is reported to have confirmed the wreck is in six major sections, the result of destructive collapse (fragmentation) 6000 feet above the sea-floor.

Note: the depth value (2400 feet) and energy yield (22,500 pounds of TNT) of the THRESHER collapse event were derived using the empiric relationship between the volume of a collapsing structure and the bubble-pulse frequency discussed on page 134 of the WINTER 2012 issue of THE SUBMARINE REVIEW. The formula is provided on page C4 of Naval Ordnance Laboratory letter serial 69-160 of 20 January 1970, USS SCORPION (SSN 589) RESULTS OF NOL DATA ANALYSIS (U).

APPENDIX B

Why the Legacy of the SCORPION Court of Inquiry is Misinformation

Monograph of 27 April 2015

Subj: Why the Legacy of the SCORPION Court of Inquiry is Misinformation

DISCUSSIONS:

With the approach of the end of the 47th year since the loss of the USS SCORPION at 18:42:34Z on 22 May 1968, it is appropriate to review the major erroneous conclusion reached by the SCORPION Court of inquiry. Their basic conclusion was wrong because they listened to the wrong person {John Craven) and ignored the right persons: their own team of experts, the Structural Analysis Group {SAG): Peter Palermo, CAPT Harry Jackson and Robert Price.

Basically, John Craven {1924-2015) convinced the Court of Inquiry that a Bubble Pulse Frequency {BPF) created by a structural collapse event could be "swallowed" within the collapsing structure and not be acoustically detected. As stated earlier, the problem with that assertion is that any structure that is collapsed by hydrostatic pressure - the SCORPION pressure-hull in this case - is destroyed by the initial compression phase of the collapse event; therefore, there is no intact structure remaining within which the BPF can be "swallowed." It propagates freely to enormous detection ranges limited only by the bathymetry of the ocean area in which it occurs.

That erroneous "swallowing" conclusion transmogrified into the Court Inquiry assessment that SCORPION was lost because of the "explosion of a large charge weight external to the pressure-hull" which provided the basis for the conspiracy theorists to conjecture Soviet complicity in the disaster.

The SAG - based on the results of microscopic, spectrographic and X-ray diffraction analyses of recovered battery components by Portsmouth Naval Shipyard personnel - and analysis of acoustic data - correctly concluded SCORPION was lost because hydrogen out-gassed by the main battery had exploded before there was any flooding of the battery well. The SAG also concluded that collapse of the SCORPION pressure-hull had produced a strong BPF. Basically, the SAG had the right answers but their input was dismissed by the Court of Inquiry.

Compounding its erroneous conclusions, the Court of Inquiry failed to examine acoustic detections of the collapse of the USS THRESHER on 10 April 1963, an event that produced a BPF detected at a range of 1300 nautical miles with a signal to background noise ratio of about 30 dB, sufficient to have been detected to ranges at least equal to the circumference of the Earth had there been an unobstructed, deep-water signal transmission path: no bathymetric occlusion. It is difficult to understand how this egregious oversight by the Court of Inquiry could have occurred but regardless of why it occurred, it remains the pivotal mistake responsible for misinformation still in the public domain about the loss of SCORPION which the Navy has never acknowledged and publicly corrected.

Fourteen of the SCORPION Court of Inquiry's 17 basic conclusions were wrong. In baseball parlance, that's a batting average of .176.

John Craven may have convinced the Court of Inquiry but not the Navy's Bureau of Ships who, in turn, dismissed the Court of Inquiry external explosion conclusion; accepted the SAG battery-explosion assessment, and, only 10 months after the loss of SCORPION, issued new directives on "Safety Aspects of Battery Ventilation" and "Inspection During Battery Charge." (NAVSHIPS Technical MANUAL, Chapters 9623.721 and 9623.718, March 1969 Edition.)

Below are the bona fides of the three members of the SAG whose conclusion the SCORPION Court of Inquiry chose to ignore in favor of John Craven whose experience/knowledge in the relevant technical areas was "limited."

1. Peter M. Palermo (1929-2009), 1984 recipient Gold Medal Award for his significant contribution to naval engineering as set forth in the following:

"For outstanding technical achievement and leadership as a naval architect and structural engineer of international reputation specializing in the demanding technology of submarine pressure hulls.

"Mr. Palermo's exceptional contributions have encompassed all facets of submarine hull structure development, design, fabrication and maintenance. His development of structural design criteria has provided the Navy with unique capabilities for producing the most structurally efficient submarine pressure hulls in the world. This capability affords the Navy the opportunity to devote a maximum portion of the ship's displacement to mission systems. Mr. Palermo utilized these capabilities in the structural design of the Los Angeles and Trident class submarines. His exceptional technical knowledge of structural fabrication has provided a sound base for developing and implementing fabrication procedures which reduce construction costs while maintaining quality. His efforts in advancing the state of the art in the employment of high strength materials for submarine pressure hulls were vital to the introduction of HY-100 and HY-130 steels. In these programs, Mr. Palermo coordinated the original fracture testing and the final delivery of materials for required applications he also developed the design criteria unique to these materials and went on to develop a qualified industrial base. He thereby demonstrated that the capability existed in the U.S. shipbuilding industry to fabricate submarine structures using the new materials.

Mr. Palermo's numerous contributions will assure the safety and superiority of future U.S. Submarines.

2. CAPT Harry A. Jackson, USN (1916-2005) recipient Harold E. Saunders Award for his significant contribution to naval engineering as set forth in the following quotes: "Combining his experience in the nuclear power program with the success of the single-screw Attack Submarine, Captain Jackson led the design and development of the deep diving, SSN 594 Class Submarines. This stands as the greatest advancement in performance and capability yet achieved in a single new class design. His design and engineering expertise were crucial factors in the successful development of the Fleet Ballistic Missile Submarine that currently is one of the Nation's primary strategic defense systems."

As further discussed in CAPT Jackson's award certificate: "In his post-active duty career, Captain Jackson continues to direct his talents and expertise toward improving submarine design and engineering: as an advisor and counselor to Navy management; as an engineering consultant; and most importantly, as a teacher, passing on his expertise and experience to future Engineering Duty Officers and civilian engineers. The soundness of his personal contributions have stood well the test or time. and his continuing service and teaching of those who will follow him augur well for the future. The Society therefore considers him most worthy of being recognized and is honored to present him with its Harold E. Saunders Award for 1979."

3. Robert Price: it need only be said that when, in 1974, ADM H. G. Rickover was looking for an expert in the effects of underwater explosions to investigate the loss of the USS MAINE in Havana Harbor in 1898, he chose Robert Price who had worked for the Navy in the field of underwater explosions for 25 years; had studied the loss of Navy ships, and had conducted many explosive tests. In 1974, Robert Price published "SOUNDS FROM IMPLOSIONS OF STEEL CYLINDERS UNDER WATER" (NOLTR 74-168), Naval Ordnance Laboratory, White Oak, Maryland, 20 September 1974, and Naval Ordnance Laboratory Report ADA-000-807 of 29 Sep 1974

APPENDIX C

Discussion of the Temporal and Dynamic Characteristics
of the Collapse of the USS SCORPION Pressure-Hull

Monograph of 26 March 2017

Subj: Discussion of the Temporal and Dynamic Characteristics of the Collapse of the USS SCORPION Pressure-Hull

BACKGROUND

Extensive imagery obtained of the SCORPION wreck by the US submersible TRIESTE confirmed that the engine room had symmetrically "telescoped" 50-feet forward when the cone-to-cylinder transition junction failed between the auxiliary machine space and the engine room. The propeller shaft- with the propeller still attached -was found to have separated from the after section of the wreck.

Whether loss of the propeller shaft caused the loss of SCORPION or was the result of collapse of the pressure-hull at great depth has been a subject of continuing debate.

Analysis of acoustic detections of the SCORPION collapse event acoustic signal has resolved this issue.

DISCUSSIONS

Analysis of the acoustic detection of the bubble-pulse signal created by the collapse of the intact SCORPION pressure-hull confirm the duration of the collapse phase of that event - which occurred at a depth of 1530-feet (680 psi) - was 1/271h of a second (0.037 seconds). The velocity of a collapsing (telescoping) after hull sections was about 900 mph: 50-feet in 0.037 seconds. The velocity of the intruding water-ram which produced that compressive force was 2000 mph.

It was this enormous axially-aligned forward vector - opposed (primarily) by inertial forces (a body at rest tends to stay at rest) acting on both the shaft and the propeller, and (secondarily) by the resistance of the water acting on the effective blade area of the propeller that tore the shaft - with the propeller still attached - from the thrust block and out of the submarine where it fell separately to the bottom to be imaged near the telescoped after hull sections by TRIESTE.

Imagery also showed the retention flange of the shaft was separated from the body of the shaft. Basically, the after sections of the SCORPION accelerated forward (away from) the propeller and its attached shaft at 900 mph leaving the unsupported shaft to sink to the bottom where it was imaged in proximity to the after-sections of the hull.

This assessment resolves the long-standing issue: was loss of the propeller shaft the cause or the result of the loss of the USS SCORPION? It was the result of the collapse of the pressure-hull.

An alternate explanation - that the propeller had lost ("thrown") a blade and the resulting imbalance separated the shaft- is rejected.

SUPPORTING ANALYSIS

Invalidation of the assumption that the initial compression and expansion (rebound) phases of the collapse of a submarine pressure-hull at great depth are symmetrical (of equal duration), and measurement of the acoustic signal (bubble pulse) created by the collapse-expansion cycle of air within the SCORPION pressure-hull indicate SCORPION collapsed (complete destruction: fragmentation/ compression) in one-sixth of the reciprocal of the bubble-pulse frequencies of 4.46 Hz or in 0.037 seconds.

Temporal asymmetry exists between the compression and expansion phases of the bubble-pulse signal produced by submarine pressure-hull collapse events because the duration of the collapse phase is truncated by the collapse phase pressure wave encountering the compacting mass of the hull and internal structures whereas the expansion (rebound) phase terminates less abruptly when the falling pressure of that expanding wave and its momentum are overcome by the ambient pressure at the collapse depth.

APPENDIX D
Extracts From An Analytic and Numerical
Study of Underwater Implosions

Title of Source Article: Analytic and Numerical Study of Underwater Implosions, June 2013

Author: Lynn Andrew Gish

Document Source: Archives Massachusetts Institute of Technology.

Dissemination note from the document: "The author hereby grants to MIT permission to reproduce and to distribute publicly paper and electronic copies of this thesis document in whole or in part in any medium now known or hereafter created."

Readers are encouraged to access the source document and read it in its entirety.

DISCUSSIONS:

The underwater implosion problem was analyzed using an energy balance approach, with the principle of virtual velocities as a foundation. The primary goal of the research was to develop tools and methods to accurately estimate the severity of an implosion pulse (quantified by the pulse energy), given a cylinder geometry, material properties, and external hydrostatic pressure. A secondary goal was to apply the knowledge gained through the research to make design recommendations to minimize the implosion severity.

Underwater implosion refers to the rapid collapse of a solid structural shell resulting from fluid loading. Implosion occurs when the hydrostatic pressure exceeds the critical buckling pressure of the structure, or through a combination of hydrostatic pressure less than critical buckling pressure and a triggering event, such as an underwater explosive load. The duration of a typical implosion event is on the order of milliseconds. (Depending of the diameter of the imploding cylinder, maximum internal pressure can occur within one-half millisecond of the time of the initial structural beach.)

The negative phase represents the decrease in pressure due to the collapsing cylinder walls and the associated in-rushing water. The large positive spike is caused by the rapid deceleration (and subsequent compression) of the water when the structure reaches its maximum collapse and stops moving. (Author's note: this "spike" was observed in the SCORPION acoustic data 37 milliseconds after the initial rise in signal level (start of the collapse event) and exceeded any noise-level previously detected during the collapse phase.)

Urick observed that the energy transmitted in an implosion pulse was significantly less than that of an oscillating gas bubble of equivalent size. This observation indicated that a significant amount of energy is absorbed by the deformation and fracture of the collapsing structure

The pressure-time histories show a negative pressure phase corresponding to the cylinder surface accelerating away from the water (i.e., collapsing), followed by a positive pressure phase corresponding to the cylinder surface accelerating toward the water (or equivalently, the surface coming to rest and the water decelerating against it). The sharp positive pressure spike corresponds generally to the moment of contact between the two sides of the cylinder.

Price observed that cylindrical implosions generally exhibit only a single negative and positive pressure phase. He concluded that the oscillation decreases as the ratio of structure to volume of enclosed air increases.

Price also experimented with cylinders with multiple compartments and different materials. His data provides an important insight into implosion of cylinders, and the effect of features like bulkheads and stiffeners.

Most of the recent research directly related to underwater implosion has been driven by U.S. Navy interest. Cor and Miller studied spherical and cylindrical implodable volumes and the effect that energy absorption by internal structure has on the implosion pressure pulse. They concluded that internal structure can significantly reduce the implosion pressure pulse,.

The buckling mode of a cylinder subjected to hydrostatic pressure is determined by the cylinder's length (2L), diameter (D), and thickness (h), in accordance with classical elastic-plastic buckling theory.

In hydrostatically-induced implosion, the hydrostatic pressure loading on the solid body causes rapid movement of the solid surface (i.e., deformation or crushing of the body). This rapid movement of the solid surface causes corresponding motion of the adjacent fluid (because of kinematic continuity requirements), which in turn causes a local hydrodynamic pressure change (decrease) in the fluid. The changing fluid pressure acting on the solid surface changes the acceleration of the solid surface, which further changes the fluid velocity and pressure. In a typical underwater implosion, the entire collapse occurs in a few milliseconds. Thus, the implosion problem is a fully-coupled, highly dynamic and nonlinear problem.

PHASES OF COLLAPSE:

The symmetric collapse of a cylinder under hydrostatic load is divided into three phases. Phase 1 is from initiation of collapse until the moment of first contact between opposite cylinder walls. First contact occurs at a single point on the center cross-section. After first contact, the cylinder begins to flatten in both the radial direction on the center cross-section, and the longitudinal direction. Phase 2 is from the moment of first contact until the moment of maximum flattening of the center cross-section. The degree of flattening of the center cross-section is dependent on the hydrostatic pressure and the diameter-to-thickness ratio *(D/h)*. Following Phase 2, the flattening progresses longitudinally along the cylinder until it reaches a final state. Phase 3 is from the end of Phase 2 until the final state. As in Phase 2, the extent of final flattening is dependent on the hydrostatic pressure and the diameter-to- thickness ratio *(D/h)*.

LONGITUDINAL ASSUMPTIONS:

Bhat and Wierzbicki and Dyau and Kyriakides studied propagating buckles in long pipelines under hydrostatic load. They concluded that in an infinitely long unconstrained pipeline, a localized region of deformation (i.e., buckling) occurs, and the deformation zone then travels in both directions along the length of the pipe.

In contrast, the present analysis of finite-length cylinders with rigid endcaps under hydrostatic load indicates that deformation occurs along the entire length of the cylinder, even in the earliest stages. There is no traveling or expanding longitudinal deformation zone. (Author's note: imagery of the Israeli submarine DAKAR – lost in the Mediterranean in January 1968 – showed such a linear deformation (breach) along almost the entire length of the hull.)

These results indicate that the difference in longitudinal behavior reported for pipelines and that observed in the present work may be explained primarily by the presence of trigger loads or imperfections. If a trigger load or impetfection is present, the deformation will begin at that location and travel longitudinally, as observed in long pipelines. If no imperfections or trigger loads are present, the deformation will occur along the entire length and will be greatest at the center of the cylinder.

The actual air compression during implosion is likely somewhere between isothermal and adiabatic. Because the implosion event happens so rapidly, it is reasonable to assume that very little heat will transfer across the cylinder boundary and the process is closer to adiabatic than isothermal. Therefore, adiabatic compression is assumed throughout the remainder of this work.

During implosion, the cylinder structural walls rapidly collapse until they contact the opposite wall and motion stops. As the structure collapses, the surrounding fluid accelerates to follow the structure. The moving fluid creates a dynamic pressure in the vicinity of the cylinder that is negative in sign. The dynamic pressure adds to the constant hydrostatic pressure to give the total fluid pressure acting on the sutface.

The kinetic energy continues to increase slightly beyond the end of Phase 1, because portions of the cylinder are still accelerating inward even though the center section has stopped.

This is no longer the case once the first contact occurs between cylinder walls (i.e., after Phase 1). When contact occurs, the structural motion abruptly stops and the fluid rapidly decelerates and compresses. This compression of the fluid causes a high pressure wave which propagates away from the cylinder (i.e., the implosion pulse).

Acoustic analysts are encouraged to acquire and carefully study SOUNDS FROM IMPLOSIONS OF STEEL CYLINDERS UNDER WATER (NOLTR 74-168) by Robert S. Price, Naval Ordnance Laboratory, White Oak, Maryland, 20 September 1974.

In 1968. Price was a member of the SCORPION Structural Analysis Group and the Navy's leading authority on the effects of underwater explosions and implosions.

Epilogue: A Less Technical Summary of
Why the USS THRESHER Was Lost

Submarines are ballasted to be neutrally buoyant with zero trim so the weight of the submarine equals the weight of the water it displaces.

As the depth of a submarine increases, sea pressure also increases compressing the pressure-hull which increases the "effective" weight of the submarine by reducing the displacement while the weight remains constant.

The submarine becomes increasingly negatively buoyant with depth and will sink at an increasing rate unless its effective weight is reduced by pumping water overboard, an operation called "compensation."

If compensation procedures are not followed, a submarine with the pressure-hull volume of THRESHER will effectively gain about 1000 pounds of weight for every 100 feet of increased depth because of hull compression.

As long as the speed of a submarine is above about four knots, that speed and the effect of control surfaces (dive planes) can hold a submarine at a selected depth even if it is significantly heavy (negatively buoyant), a condition that may not be apparent to the crew.

Analysis of acoustic data confirms that after losing propulsion because of a nuclear reactor shut-down - with the consequent loss of speed, THRESHER sank from a depth of 1300-feet to collapse 9.5 minutes later at a depth of 2400-feet for an average sink-rate of about 120 feet a minute.

As discussed in detail by Chapter 1, Issue A, multiple lines of evidence confirm there was no flooding of THRESHER's pressure-hull before collapse.

With the elimination of flooding, there is no explanation for the documented sink-rate other than failure to follow standard compensation procedures during the 10 April 1963 dive to 1300-feet.

Survival of the THRESHER pressure-hull without flooding before collapse at nearly twice the maximum permitted operating depth is based on the detailed analyses provided by Chapter 1. Additionally, THRESHER never reported "flooding" to her escort ship, the USS SKYLARK. Those factors - and others discussed in Chapter 1, Issue A - provide the basis for rejecting the Navy Court of Inquiry's conclusion that flooding was the cause of the disaster or, indeed, that there was any flooding at all before collapse of the pressure-hull at an extreme depth.

The Portsmouth Naval Shipyard, Kittery, ME, personnel are thus exculpated of the Navy implied complicity in the disaster because of faulty silver-brazing of a sea-connected pipe between two- and five-inches in diameter.

Loss of propulsion (reactor scram) from a still unknown cause (NOT flooding), failure to compensate for hull-compression from increasing pressure during the dive to test-depth (1300-feet), and failure of the deballasting system because of the formation of ice in the air-lines were the primary factors responsible for the loss of THRESHER.

www.ingramcontent.com/pod-product-compliance
Lightning Source LLC
Chambersburg PA
CBHW050618110426

42813CB00008B/2600